GETTING
TO KNOW WHO?

A Simple Look at the Nature of God

Barry L. Johnson

THE UPPER ROOM
NASHVILLE, TENNESSEE

GETTING
TO KNOW WHO?

The scripture quotations not otherwise identified are from the Revised Standard Version of the Bible, copyrighted 1946, 1952 and © 1971 by the Division of Christian Education, National Council of the Churches of Christ in the United States of America, and are used by permission.

The poem "Focus" by Mark Link, S. J., is from *He Is the Still Point of the Turning World* by Mark Link, S.J. © 1971 Mark Link, S. J. (Published by Argus Communications). Reprinted by permission of Argus Communications, Allen, Texas.

The poem on page 28 is from Marilee Zdenek, *God Is a Verb*, copyright © 1974; used by permission of Word Books, Publisher, Waco, Texas 76796.

The excerpt on page 54 is from *Second Wind: The Memoirs of an Opinionated Man* by Bill Russell and Taylor Branch. Copyright © 1979 by William F. Russell. Reprinted by permission of Random House Inc.

The excerpt on page 63 is copyright © 1951 by John Cheever. Reprinted from *The Stories of John Cheever* by John Cheever by permission of Alfred A. Knopf Inc.

The excerpt from "The Conquest of America" by Archibald MacLeish first appeared in *The Atlantic Monthly*, August 1949, 184:17-22. Reprinted by permission of Houghton Mifflin Company.

Book Design: Patricia Bolton
First printing: September, 1981 (5)
Library of Congress Catalog Card Number: 81-52217
ISBN: 0-8358-0424-0
Printed in the United States of America

GETTING
TO KNOW WHO?

For Celeste,
whose faith enlightens mine,
whose love is my key to courage

Contents

Preface

This is a book for the eighties. It does not suffocate with self-help theory. It does not snipe at existent institutions. And it does not promise untold riches for faithful perseverance. I hope we may have passed those levels of privation.

It does challenge with concept. It does respond to old but relevant questions. And it does provide handles for days of distress. As I see it, these are the needs of the years ahead.

This all was prompted by the annual year-end sermon on *what has been*. The only difference was that this time I decided to play a game and look back ten years on one Sunday, ahead ten on the next. It was the second effort that caught me. Never having seen myself as a prophet, it was an eerie feeling to project what life for a Christian might be like in 1990. In fact, the only way to imagine such an existence was to take a hard look at the way things are now and single out those items to change . . . by choice or necessity.

One such item set my adrenalin flowing.

We have just emerged from a tremendous siege of Christian individualism. From 1970 to 1975 I was making a living on this mood while traveling about the nation doing church renewal (*Euriskon*) programs. At the heart of this ministry was a commitment to confirm the pilgrimage of every person as a child of God. At that time it was apparent that people longed for personal assurances steeped in group exchanges, encounter therapy, and testimonial writing. Lyman Coleman surfaced with *Serendipity*. Keith Miller blitzed the religious book market with *The Taste of New Wine*. Bruce Larson reeled off a whole series of readable works designed for lay people and clergy alike. Those were the days when it was refreshing to find so many people talking openly and freely about their faith.

But the pendulum moved too far and the Christian self-help movement became an end in itself. The idea survived its time and exploiters strangled its vitality. Maharishi Yogi, Sun Myung Moon, and other gurus from the East stumped America, mouths watering over the willing vulnerability of so many targets, particularly young people. Reverend Ike used riches to gain riches. Leroy Jenkins milked the healing circuit and got caught with matches in his hand. And Oral Roberts sought to build a hospital when and where the doctors said it was not needed.

It was inevitable. Questions of integrity appeared everywhere. It was as if the fallout of national cynicism prompted by Watergate and Vietnam had finally settled to the level of religion.

Right alongside this sardonic philosophy came the OPEC-induced knowledge that America was not invulnerable. We discovered we cannot have everything we want. We do not have the resources we need to sit back and thumb our noses at the rest of the world. Clay feet cracked—mine, yours, the government's, the church's.

The result is a deep-seated hunger for digestible theology. Not the high-altitude stuff of academia, but that which evolves when those conjectures are sifted through the filter of life experiences.

Getting to Know Who? is a response to that need and, I hope, a harbinger of things to come in the world of popular religious writing. I think we are ready for more serious investigations of the basics of our faith, things that are palpable as well as enlightening and entertaining.

The first section of *Getting to Know Who?* focuses on how the average person can relate his or her experiences to a supernatural God. It also introduces an approach to detecting the hand of God at work in one's life every day. When I was writing this part I got so excited about the concept that I ran out of my study, cornered three people in our office, and tried to explain the whole idea. Amid ringing phones, incoming hospital reports, the incessant thump of the mimeograph, and a mailman waiting for 25 cents postage due, they loved it. I hope you will, too.

The second section reacquaints us with the idea of
the holy. Somehow, during all that touching and
sharing, we seem to have lost the ability to stand in
awe. We have become accustomed to holding and
molding everything ourselves. The God of
Abraham, Isaac, Jacob, and Jesus defies that box.
This section denotes the power, justice, and grace of
God while challenging us to make it a regular
practice to "keep silence before him" (Hab. 2:20).

The final section is a bugle blast to deal
responsibly with the trauma of the present and the
possibilities of the future. I believe we are looking to
a decade when religious beliefs will become
increasingly important, not only in the church but
in all our major institutions, including the realm of
politics.

I have sought to concentrate on the practical
issues common to believers and nonbelievers as well.
Throughout the book, I have used the masculine
pronoun when referring to God. This is in no way
a statement about the nature of God, for scripture
points out aspects of God that are both traditionally
feminine and traditionally masculine. The image of
God as containing these qualities is a deep
theological issue that cannot be dealt with
completely within the pages of this book. A
masculine pronoun is used, therefore, for clarity of
communication. Those readers who are sensitive to
the use of male pronouns referring to God may read

"he/she" or "she/he" when "he" refers to God.

I would like to thank all the people who contributed to my writing effort. Most notably, my wife and children, who survived the gestation period; my staff (particularly Gary Hogue and Bill Hensley), who covered the bases for me so I could hibernate and compose; and my friends Donovan and Mary Herres, who so graciously loaned me the use of their cottage so I could brood and do without interruption.

Barry L. Johnson
Artist Island
Indian Lake, Ohio
1980

GETTING
TO KNOW WHO?

I.
Far and Near:
A Look at Our Sovereign Creator

Philosophy of Religion 238. It was a 200 course, an elective. During the mid to late sixties it seemed to lose its importance. Twice it was postponed for a semester due to a lack of interest. Then came the seventies with Watergate, Jimmy Carter, and a renewal of spiritual consciousness. Suddenly 238 was filled. Apparently, students couldn't get enough of it.

So now the professor sat with her favorite project before her. It always baffled the students, or so they said. It also provided insight into their bias—an insight not attainable in any other way. She always did it the third week. No special reason. Perhaps because, by then, they were settled down with her style. They trusted her. Hence, she would pass out the sketch pads and issue the instructions: "Today, there will be no lecture. You will be given the entire period to complete this assignment. Please turn in your paper as you leave the room. Draw God."

The response this year was similar to the response

for the past fifteen; first, laughter; then,
bewilderment; and finally, silence as they set
themselves to the task.

Given the same instructions right now . . . what
would you do? Consider some of the responses:

—a pot-bellied man with a handlebar mustache, a
   brass-buttoned vest, striped trousers, a walking
   stick, and a big cigar;

—a perfect circle with a solitary dot in the center;

—a facsimile of Michelangelo's masterpiece in the
   Sistine Chapel: an ephemeral creature issuing
   from a cloud with the head of a man, a long
   flowing beard, and a perfectly detailed arm
   reaching forth as if to touch.

And always the biblical backgrounds unveiled
themselves:

—a burning bush;

—a whirling cloud;

—an illuminating burst of light;

—and, of course, the cross.

But the impact of this experiment perennially
produced a common conclusion. We know very
little about God. And what we do know is tragically
confined within a cultural box over which we
maintain total control.

—Who is God?

—How does God reveal himself to us?

—Can we relate to God?

—What are God's attributes?

And how, if at all, does God make any difference in the quality of our lives?

Getting to Know Who? responds to these questions and more. They are not new questions. Theologians have addressed them for hundreds of years. But unfortunately they have rarely been approached in common terms. Undoubtedly this is due to the expansive nature of the questions. Simply in terms of vocabulary they present a formidable challenge. *Omniscience, pantheism,* and *teleology* are not words commonly dropped in the barbershop or at bridge club, or even in a service of worship. They belong to theologians. And they should stay with theologians.

I will do everything I can to avoid professional jargon. Given the opportunity, I shall employ parables instead of syllables, because the relationship between God and God's children is, at root, simple. Let's keep it that way. Maybe, among the three of us . . . you, me, and our subject . . . we can paint some pictures that will answer some questions that will change some opinions that will enrich some lives. Is that too much to ask? I hope not. It is the goal.

TOO CLOSE FOR COMFORT

Not long ago I heard a story about a fellow who had been invited to a Christian Encounter Retreat. Although he wasn't too crazy about "therapizing"

with people he had never met, he went anyhow. It
proved to be exactly what he feared it would be—an
exercise in humanizing God and deifying humans.
As he turned to leave he was confronted with a
huge poster that summed up the whole problem. It
read: "God Is Other People!" The man could
endure no longer. Abruptly seizing a magic marker
while many of the participants looked on, he placed
a comma between the words *other* and *people*.

It is my feeling that any serious discussion of the
nature of God must start right there. I have had my
fill of God-shrink brought about by sharing groups.
It may well be healthy for people spontaneously to
share feelings with and about each other. But, from
my point of view, it belittles the Almighty to
assume

—God can be no stronger than a prayer
   partner.

—God can be no more compassionate than a
   friendly listener.

—And God can be no more skilled than a T-
   group enabler.

God is not other people. God is Other, people!

Can it be more clear than in the words of
Isaiah?

> Seek the Lord while he may be found. . . .
> For my thoughts are not your thoughts,
>   neither are your ways my ways, says the Lord.

> For as the heavens are higher than the earth,
>   so are my ways higher than your ways
>   and my thoughts than your thoughts.
>
> Isaiah 55:6*a*,8,9

So if God is not just an ideal derived from fallout of the human model, then what is God?

THE MASTER OF TEMPO

God is *sovereign.*

As such, God possesses supreme power. God can do whatever he chooses to do. Early in my ministry I was frequently confronted with the effects of the charismatic movement. The question was always the same. The intent varied. "Do you believe the Holy Spirit can give the gift of tongues?" If the questioner was charismatic, I was being set up to secure a position. If not, I was expected to crack a foundation. I always answered the same way, flippant though it may seem. "I believe the Holy Spirit can turn you into a grapefruit if he chooses." I do. But I also believe God unfolds his plan with respect for his children and a concern for harmony in the world. Still, God holds the power to do whatever he chooses.

Now, at this point we frequently collide with the game players. They delight in piecing together insurmountable problems.

—Can God create a rock so big he can't move it?

—Can God destroy himself?

—Do the acts of humans defeat the will of God?

In responding to such semantic snares, we must be reminded that though God is not controlled by the way we relate to him, *God chooses to be controlled by the way he relates to us.*

Perhaps the best way to explain this is to call attention to William James's description of the interaction between a father, who is a master chess player, and a son, who is a novice. When the two indulge in a game, the father controls the pace. He is such a superior player that he can determine the style of the game. He doesn't control the son—he doesn't want to. He wants the son to learn and grow and make decisions on his own. Although he holds the power to win or lose in a minute, his relationship to the boy causes him to modulate his dominion in respect for the freedom of his son. God's sovereignty works the same way with us. God can do whatever he pleases. But God's choices are defined, as we discover in the Bible, by his covenantal relationship with his people.

He is not like the first-day patrol boy who caused twenty-six schoolmates to be late to class because he held them at the curb until a car passed. God doesn't use power just because he has it. And that, in itself, is a tremendous mark of his sovereignty.

BEYOND BOUNDARIES

Another mark of God's freedom from external control, or sovereignty, is the fact that we cannot locate the Almighty as an object among objects. We cannot limit God's existence by defining his being.

Recently the rage among scientists has been the study of the human brain. We are discovering phenomenal truths about the power of mind over matter. All this is possible because of laboratory experiments—containable, observable, measurable study of the brain as an entity unto itself. Because we can define it, restrict its environment, isolate its action, we can control it and, one day, thoroughly understand it.

Many people do the same with God. Theirs seems to be the calling to package the Father in a neat container perfectly suited for human observation and study. And we help them when we tie our faith to a single medium of expression.

This is what is wrong with binding God to the sensitivity training scene. We might learn something about God through studying human feelings, but such feelings simply aren't big enough to contain God entirely. God works there but he doesn't live there.

This is what is wrong with basing all theology on the scripture. The greatest supply of data regarding the divine-human encounter is found in the Bible, but it is not big enough to contain God entirely.

The Bible is a static record of holy history. God is
alive and well and living in Dayton . . . and
Chicago . . . and Los Angeles . . . and Detroit. The
scripture shares his truth. God works there but he
doesn't live there.

And this is what is wrong with seeking to hold
God to the revelation in Christ. Though God was
in Christ making peace with the world, the
historical figure of our Lord is too small to contain
all the nature and attributes of God. Christ gives us
unmistakable insight to the love of God, but he
does not totally define God. To be sure, we come to
the Father through the Son. As the Master so
clearly explained to Philip, we can know God
through Christ. But God is not completely defined
in Christ. God works there but he doesn't live
there.

Emil Brunner, the Swiss theologian, made this
same point by referring to the "mystery of God."

> All that we can know is the world. God is not the world.
> Therefore He is also exalted above all our knowledge. He
> is Mystery. Not simply a riddle, for riddles can be solved
> eventually—some sooner, some later. That God is
> mystery means that *we* cannot solve the enigma.[1]

I like to compare this to the phrase so often
linked to the marriage rite: "and the two became
one." It sounds magnificent. And when the couple
symbolizes it by using two candles to ignite a third

after which the first two are extinguished, it is a beautiful moment indeed. Almost holy. It is also baloney! No two ever become one. Person cannot be absorbed by person.

They can get pretty close together. Maybe that is why the Bible chooses to describe the very closest of human relationships as the process of "knowing" one another. But even that knowing is not all-inclusive. In every person there are unrevealed corners never to be understood by anyone.

Thus, if it is impossible to totally *know* another human being, it only stands to reason that we shall never totally *know* God!

> For my thoughts are not your thoughts,
>   neither are your ways my ways.
>   Isaiah 55:8

—God is Other.
—God is the Master of our tempo.
—God is beyond boundaries.
—So if we have no hope of fully comprehending God, why bother?

DIVINE AND DELIBERATE DISCLOSURE

We cannot know God totally; we *can know* as much as he reveals to us. And every day he shows new portions of his character in myriad ways.

—God comes to us in the silent fury of a rising sun.

—God comes to us in the innocent trust of the eyes of a child.

—God comes to us in the inclusive touch of a special friend.

—God comes to us in both the historical Jesus and our living Lord.

—God comes to us in prayer.

Mark Link, a Jesuit priest who personifies the fruits of monasticism, describes the challenge this presents to us.

God is like space.
He permeates all reality.
And like space,
his presence is so pervasive
that we tend to overlook it
or take it for granted.

But God does more
than permeate reality.
He also uses created reality
as the vehicle of communication
with man.

If we are to find God
and communicate with him,
we must look for him in the world
and we must discover him
in the events of daily life.

Prayer might be compared
to what happens
when we tune a TV set.

> Tuning merely brings into focus
> signals that are already present.
>
> Prayer is our point of contact, focus,
> and communication with God.[2]

This is the final aspect of his sovereignty, the will to impart himself. God wants us to live in increasing knowledge of him. God actively pursues a relationship with each of us as individuals. God makes certain that "signals," as Link puts it, are out there. He gives us unceasing opportunities to realize his love and establish a continuing relationship with him.

He comes to us.

> Whither shall I go from thy Spirit?
>   Or whither shall I flee from thy presence?
> If I ascend to heaven, thou art there!
>   If I make my bed in Sheol, thou art there!
> If I take the wings of the morning
>   and dwell in the uttermost parts of the sea,
> even there thy hand shall lead me,
>   and thy right hand shall hold me.
>   Psalm 139:7–10

We cannot escape God, so we may as well begin to know him. After all, that's the way God wants it . . . and that's the way we need it.

In this light, that which seems so far away suddenly draws near.

THE BEAT GOES ON

It's the eighth day that bothers me. On the first
God made light and darkness. On the third he
made vegetation. On the fifth he made swarms of
living creatures. And on the seventh he rested. But
what happened on the eighth day?

For most of us that is a thought rarely
entertained. We consider the magnitude of all God
did in six days and assume that he retired
undefeated. Such an assumption numbs us to the
continuing work of a caring God.

He didn't quit. A strong case can be made for the
idea that the whole act of creation was to develop
an arena where his majesty, love, and power might
reign forever. Creation did not conclude with a
potluck supper on the seventh day. It continues.
God is still at work. Here. Now.

One day while I was browsing in a bookstore, I
found a book by two very talented women, entitled
God Is a Verb! When I saw it, I stopped in my
tracks. I already had a handful of books, but I
placed them all on the floor and began to peruse
the poetry and pictures of this fascinating little
book.

I knew I had a winner in my hand when I read
the title poem by Marilee Zdenek:

> You are the healing
> the loving
> the touching

> You are the laughing
> You are the dancing
>
> Jesus, Verb of God
> You are the moving—
>   move in me.[3]

No, God did not quit on the seventh day. Creation is his masterpiece. But, like any true artist, he knows masterpieces are always unfinished, always under development. Anyone who has ever created anything knows this. Whether it's a cabinet or a painting or a novel—the creator always knows its weaknesses and, given the opportunity, he will continue to tinker with the project as long as it is in his hands.

Creation is an ongoing process. What we have is marvelous. But be assured, God is in the act of making it even better every day.

Paul Tillich captured this truth in just three sentences.

> The doctrine of creation is not the story of an event which took place "once upon a time." It is the basic description of the relation between God and the world. . . . God *has* created the world, he *is* creative in the present moment, and he *will* creatively fulfill his *telos* [ultimate end or object].[4]

WHAT'S HAPPENING NOW

It is the action of God in the present that is so important to us. This is the *now* generation. We are accustomed to instant everything. From two-minute

coffee to quantitative analysis on hand-held
calculators, from time-capsuled cold remedies to
electronic rhythm sections on color-keyed home
organs, we have learned to be children of the
moment. Yesterday was quaint and tomorrow could
be catastrophic, but our number one concern is
how to get the most out of *today*.

The recent book by a former employee of one of
America's leading religious television evangelists
exposes the way this mind-set can be manipulated.
These are the characters who use the airwaves to
build kingdoms for themselves; they are the volume
dealers for Jesus. A portion of the book focuses on
the secret to tallying wealth through the television
audience. According to this insider, asking for help
is not the secret, needing the help is not the secret,
and demanding the help is not the secret. If you
want Americans to respond to you, there is only
one way. Promise them something *now!* It doesn't
matter what it is—olive oil for home anointing
services, a piece of burlap supposedly stained with
the blood of Christ, even a common, ordinary nail
as a symbol of suffering—just tell them it will be
there within two weeks and get out the coffer. The
coffer will soon be filled.

As I see it, this is a direct fallout of the age of
narcissism. So adept at indulging ourselves, we have
reached the point where we can't consume quickly
enough to satisfy our hunger for self-generated

affirmation. We've lost the capacity to dub ourselves superior. Our excesses have caught up with us. We have come full circle to the point where we are now in the process of forfeiting all the benefits of an interdependent society. We need "things" to blind us to our emptiness.

Dr. Aaron Stern describes our current condition in his work Me, The Narcissistic American.

> Man is not born with the capacity to love others. At birth the human infant is essentially a self-centered animal with no interest in or awareness of objects outside himself. His world contains but one inhabitant. Within this singular world he is governed solely by a drive to do his own thing, to fulfill his every need. Immediately.[5]

Is that not a perfect description of the average, hard-driving, up-the-ladder, achiever of today? But the greatest treasure of all is available every day, and a good majority of God's children never even notices it. Not just the unchurched miss this gift. Those who pride themselves on their strong faith likewise blind themselves to the ready availability of this life-changing legacy.

You see, if God is still in the process of creating (and I believe he is), then you and I are a vital part of the program. We are partners in providence.

THE MOMENT OF TRUTH

In the world of chemistry there is a word that makes my point. The word is *katalysis*. (The dictionary gives the option of spelling the word with a "c" or a "k." I choose the latter to emphasize the special significance of the word in this context.) The Funk and Wagnall definition is as follows:

> Katalysis: an increase in the rate of chemical reaction, caused by the presence of a substance that is not permanently altered by the reaction.

In other words, katalysis is change caused by contact with a party that does not change.

I see this as a flawless description of God's creative involvement with each of us. To be sure, our lives are dominated by moments of katalysis.

This may well be the most important concept in "getting to know who." When we acknowledge the ongoing creativity of God, we concurrently open ourselves to the continuing revelation of truth.

It works like this: God, through the working of the Holy Spirit, orchestrates our lives. All cohesion, balance, and direction are born of this orchestration.

One of my favorite thoughts is, "God knows your name and he knows your needs." I use it all the time, particularly when I am dealing with people in distress. It is my way of indicating that God is a part of both our needs and our names. He owns both. He is actively creating your world and he is actively creating mine. Today. Right now. Immediately.

In this capacity God leads us to and through moments of katalysis. These are those precious instances when all of God's word intersects with the life of a given individual. They are the times when the scripture as we know it, Christ as we understand him, the culture in which we live, and our individuality come together in a moment of unmistakable truth. The more we know about all these sources, the more receptive we shall be to moments of katalysis.

For some people this happens in hospital rooms when the doctor's report seems to crystalize the meaning of life and the whole package of God's love and our lives rises above any physical dilemma.

But it doesn't have to be a period of crisis for a moment of katalysis to arise. It often happens to me when I'm driving my car. In fact, it's almost a foregone conclusion if I am to drive for more than an hour by myself. In that isolated atmosphere all things suddenly seem more clear, more meaningful, more manageable! Under such circumstances new truth, for me, is a common consequence.

It can be for you, too. In fact, it is. If you fail to recognize this it is not because it is not true but rather due to lack of perception. I think of the cute play on words often employed by children when, holding their hands at their hips like a true gunslinger, they ask, "Want to see my quick draw?" Answered affirmatively, they don't even move their hands but question further, "Want to see it again?" So it is with the creativity of God. By the time we recognize a moment of katalysis the deed is complete. It is a mystical event bound over to the involved individual.

Leslie Weatherhead's explanation of the folly of seeking to prove the existence of God can be equally applied to the challenge to prove a moment of katalysis.

> There *is* no authority for God's existence except the inward conviction that is born of mystical experience. And to prove the existence of God is a bit like proving that your wife loves you, with all the same difficulties of rebutting one who says she does not really love you, but acts the way she does because life is easier for both that way, or she wants you to like her, or hopes you will leave her your money![6]

I believe this is what Mark Link refers to when he tells us prayer is a way of "tuning" God's already existent signals. God is constantly communicating with us, and when we properly receive his signals, his word (or truth) is born in us.

Solomon conveys the same thought.

> Trust in the Lord with all your heart,
>   and do not rely on your own insight.
> In all your ways acknowledge him,
>   and he will make straight your paths.
>   Proverbs 3:5,6

Is there a more poetic description of the ongoing work of a Creator God?

THE SAME YESTERDAY, TODAY, AND FOREVER

But an aspect of this process of katalysis must be underscored. Though God perpetually institutes change in our lives, he does not change. He prompts the reaction but avoids its permanent consequences. This does not mean God does not react to our deeds. He does. He is a sensitive and compassionate God. But when it comes to creativity, we must be reminded that God is the initiator and not the result. God is not changed by process. We are.

BEHOLD, THE OLD HAS PASSED AWAY. THE NEW HAS COME.

Pablo Picasso once observed that every act of creation is first of all an act of destruction. I couldn't agree more. To make something new we must do away with what is old. This is the law of regeneration. The new car replaces the old one. The new house supplants the old one. The Christian repents or turns away from a life of sin.

Likewise, in the world of art, a truly creative piece is never an exact duplicate of another. If it were, it would not be considered creative.

Thus, when we become dogmatic about our faith, we declare a moratorium on moments of katalysis for ourselves. He who refuses to change, to destroy, also refuses to grow.

When we deny all sources of revelation save the written word of God, we qualify katalysis and kill creativity.

When we hinder alterations in the church by claiming, "We've always done it this way!" we qualify katalysis and kill creativity. When we deny our mortality by surrounding ourselves with titles, tributes, treasures, and trinkets, we qualify katalysis and kill creativity.

Qualified katalysis is manipulated mediocrity. It is refusing to receive the fullness of life as God gives it. It is limiting the power of God to the perception of humankind. It is stupid.

THE ULTIMATE MOMENT OF KATALYSIS

In his Pulitzer Prize winning book *The Denial of Death*, Ernest Becker puts forth the theory that virtually all the deeds of humans are motivated by a drive to flee from our finite condition. We avoid the fact that death is unavoidable.

We amass fortunes in pursuit of immortality. We build ideologies to secure life systems. We name things after ourselves to cling to eternity. We write books, like this one, to help us live forever. And it is all a confession of our ignorance of our creator God.

If God's creativity continues, if we are partners in

providence, if God knows our names and knows
our needs, if God's word is born of contact with his
children, if our very existence is a part of a divine
destiny—if *all* these things are true, then death is
the ultimate moment of katalysis! It is the final
destruction preceding the consummate act of
creation, not something from which to hide, not
something to fear, and not something to avoid at all
cost, but something which, encountered within the
orchestration of God, should be welcomed in
triumph!

A careful explanation is in order when I say,
"encountered within the orchestration of God." I
believe God's plan for each person includes both life
and death. If life is cut short in pursuit of the
"ultimate moment of katalysis," then that moment
will lose some of its brilliance. God has charge of
life as well as death. Hence, only the fool would
consider interrupting the full course of God's
providence for himself. Suicide is a tragic mode of
escape, showing a lack of confidence in the inclusive
love of God. Christ was serious when he said, "I
came that they may have life, and have it
abundantly" (John 10:10b). At the same time the
message of the vacant tomb of Joseph of Arimathea
remains—death is not an end but a beginning.

A former classmate put this in perspective for me
when he answered my question, "What do you
think of healing in our time?" with these words:

"Barry, Christians will come a long way when they finally recognize death is God's ultimate form of healing."

We have a commanding message of the Christ who lived among us. It is not that life is better if we are kind to one another, although he did teach that; not that sacrifice is the symbol of success, although he illustrated that; and not that obedience to God is the avenue to self acceptance, although he substantiated that. No, the commanding message of Jesus Christ is that death is but a step along the way, a transition from the finite pain and problems of this temporary world to the infinite joy and opportunity of peace with God. It is the constituent act of our creator God. It is the boldest of all proclamations, the proclamation that there is more to come.

MORE TO COME

It is a great feeling to encounter truth while driving a car.

It is a comforting thought to realize that no matter how bleak a given experience might seem, God is with you. It is even more comforting to know there is more to come.

And it is an awesome challenge to observe the majesty of a mountain range, the splendor of an opening rose, and the power of a rushing wind. But it is even more challenging to observe all this as but a step along the way. There *is* more to come.

God is far from us yet so near to us. He has shown us what he can do through his Son, through his written word, through the glory of this world, through the march of history, through his very presence in our lives, and most significantly, through an empty grave. Now, we have the pleasure of living in anticipation of that ultimate moment of katalysis.

PATIENCE AND THE PROCESS

On occasion I visit Florida. When I do, I make it a habit to study people. My wife would say this is bikini-motivated; I maintain it is philanthropic. Whatever the cause, I am not a sheller. I wander the beach looking at people. God knows this, and on our most recent visit to the sunshine state he gave me a moment of katalysis in the form of a ragtag little girl. Complete with dirty face, hair askew, and a Band-Aid on one knee, she was the picture of contented catastrophe. But the real despatch was printed across her T-shirt. It made me think of McLuhan's phrase, "The medium is the message." It read, "Be patient with me, God isn't finished with me yet."

This God—so far away yet so near—becomes a good deal more real to all of us when we see ourselves in that same perspective.

The creation continues.

II.
High and Low:
A Look at Our Holy Parent

Now Moses was keeping the flock of his father-in-law,
Jethro, the priest of Midian; and he led his flock to the
west side of the wilderness, and came to Horeb, the
mountain of God. And the angel of the Lord appeared to
him in a flame of fire out of the midst of a bush; and he
looked, and lo, the bush was burning, yet it was not
consumed. And Moses said, "I will turn aside and see this
great sight, why the bush is not burnt." When the Lord
saw that he turned aside to see, God called to him out of
the bush, "Moses, Moses!" And he said, "Here am I."
Then he said, "Do not come near; put off your shoes
from your feet, for the place on which you are standing is
holy ground." And he said, "I am the God of your
father, the God of Abraham, the God of Isaac, and the
God of Jacob." And Moses hid his face, for he was afraid
to look at God.   Exodus 3:1-6.

Most humor depends on the unexpected, but not
this bit. It's funny because every viewer out there
knows what is coming next. Johnny Carson has just
completed sharing a list of things to do at parties.
And even as the talk show phenomenon concludes,
Ed McMahon, his sidekick, starts his part. First, he

asks to see the list, next he raves about its
importance, and finally he proclaims that *everything*
that ever has been written about parties is on the
list. "You are wrong, rancid fondue breath, . . ."
comes Johnny's response, and he is off into a special
list which was the main target of the whole bit from
the start. It is an amusing scene rendered more so
by the relationship between the two men. It also
contains a whimsical insight to the nature of God if
we are disposed to see it.

When McMahon says, "Everything that's ever
been written . . . ," a mechanism tripped in our
minds automatically challenges him. Not just
because we know what is coming but because we
have learned to live in the absence of absolutes.
Everything, like *never*, *always*, and *forever* just doesn't
cut it with the modern American mind.

Still, if we would discern the holiness of God, we
must commence right there. God is perfect. That is
an absolute. As such he defies management and
possession. He is *everything* and *all things* and *no
things*—summarily inconceivable to the human mind
yet unavoidable to human existence.

Perhaps the best way to engage this holiness is
through the biblical narrative involving Moses and
the burning bush. While watching over the flock of
his father-in-law, Moses is suddenly confronted with
the angel of the Lord via a bush that is burning but
not consumed. The patriarch is fascinated by this

and decides to examine it more closely. But God won't have it: "Back off, Moses, and take off your shoes. The ground on which you are standing is holy ground."

Now there are three telltale aspects of that story that give us tremendous insight into the holiness of God.

First, the bush burns but is not consumed. That is beyond our comprehension. So is the holiness of God.

Second, the bush speaks. That is beyond normal human experience. So is the holiness of God.

Third, the bush establishes its own sacred, holy zone across which Moses cannot venture. That is the whole point made clear.

A constant distance exists between God and humankind. Its measure is power. Its essence is holiness. God is holy because he cannot be held. God is holy because he thoroughly knows us even though we cannot thoroughly know him. And God is holy because he holds the power to penetrate the present and fabricate the future. Such power issues in awe.

Military people are much better at perceiving this than civilians. They live with it, in a practical sense, all the time.

A year or so ago I was invited to play a round of golf at an air force base with a young major who happened to be the base champion. I was honored

and unprepared, honored because I am not that
caliber of player and unprepared because I didn't
realize the chain of command saturates the golf
course as well as the reviewing stand.

On one particular hole I stared at the green upon
which four men were standing, and wrestled with
the notion of waiting to hit. I didn't know the
course and wasn't that sure how far away it was.
"Go ahead, preacher," came the shout from my
friend, "flail at it!"

It was his course. He should have known.

I hit one of the finest three woods I have ever hit,
and as soon as I did I heard the major exclaim, "Oh
my God, no!" With that, he sped toward the green
in the golf cart.

A large oak tree stood to the left of the green.
True to form, my direction was atrocious. The ball
rocketed into the tree and ricocheted from limb to
limb. The men on the green scattered as if a live
grenade had been pitched in their midst. I watched
dejectedly as an animated conversation ensued
between the major and one of the men who kept
gesturing back toward me as his voice echoed across
the golf course.

That scene is repeated on golf courses all over
America every golfing season. It happens. Normally,
an apology is extended and the game goes on. Not
so on this occasion. The major was a disaster for
the next sixteen holes. He played terribly, and

although he attempted to be genial and friendly, he was obviously bothered. I didn't find out until we were sitting in the officer's grill that I had smashed a golf ball into the foursome of his commanding general.

Silly as they may seem, such instances have been known to ruin distinguished careers. This is the nature of power.

Such power evokes awe and establishes distance between people. And it is not peculiar to the military world. It also exists in the worlds of athletics, business, education, and yes, the church.

We are talking about the basic difference between God as creator and God as holy. When we considered God as creator in chapter 1, we found ourselves dwelling on the way he comes to us in those wondrous moments of katalysis. When we consider God as holy, we must dwell on the manner in which we come to him.

Like the major responding to the power of the general, our mode of response to the holiness of God is a matter of subjection. The condition exists. The power is there. The question is, "How do we deal with it?"

IT'S ALL IN THE WAY YOU LOOK AT IT

Three years before the great stock market crash a German Christian by the name of Rudolf Otto wrote a book that remains a classic study of God as

holy. In the book Dr. Otto explains there are three
attributes to God's *mysterium tremendum* that
dominate his relationship with humans.

The first is *awe*, a matter of dread mixed with
veneration. The early believers removed their shoes
before entering a house of worship as a means of
displaying their vulnerability to the will of God.
Could there be a more significant gesture? Without
shoes none of us can go very far. Without shoes we
are particularly careful where we walk. And without
shoes we find ourselves humbled by the terrain
around us. This is the condition of *awe*.

The second attribute is all-inclusive *power*.
Whether it was just or not, the insulted general held
the power to alter the career of the beholden major.
Similarly, God's power, which is just, demands
respect.

Third, there is the attribute of unmeasurable
energy. God can do anything. There is no task too
great, no challenge unconquerable, and no obstacle
insurmountable. Within his being is energy
exceeding our farthest dreams.

The pattern repeats itself as we draw near to God.
Encountering the awe, power, and energy of his
holiness, we change the way we deal with him. We
experience purity.

CAN IT BE HERE?

Moses was halted in his tracks by the
announcement that the ground on which he stood

was holy; today, I am forced to wonder how
effective that announcement would be to most of
us.

Is anything holy? Do we stand in awe of any
place, person, or thing?

Again we look to Dr. Stern to analyze the
dilemma. He explains the constant drive most of us
feel to be "special." So intent are we on making a
dent in the world that we irreverently clamor after
all things that might set us apart. As a practicing
psychoanalyst, Stern reveals that the worst thing he
can say to a set of parents having tested their child
(the surest way to send those adults into depression)
is to pronounce their child "average." Nobody
wants to be average.

But the very nature of holiness dubs all people
average. Barefoot before him, every knee shall bow
as we pour contempt on all our pride.

So what has happened to our sense of holiness
today? Caught up with ourselves, we refuse to
accept the reality that no matter how much we
have developed, no matter how much nuclear
power we hold, and no matter how close we have
become to controlling the creation of life, we are
still utterly dependent on the mercy of God.

RESPECT NOTHING . . . HAVE NOTHING

Part of our problem with developing an
understanding of the holiness of God is in our
current lack of respect for nearly all forms of

authority. Convinced that all people are solely
motivated by self-aggrandizement, we don't trust
and therefore don't respect anyone—including God.

Often I spend time with the senior members of
my Shiloh Church. On one such occasion I found
myself chatting with a lady who has been a faithful
member for more than fifty years. In the course of
our conversation, she explained her concern for the
absence of respect in the sanctuary before worship.
She told of the days when, as a child, she would
help her parents clean their church and how, even
then, she felt a sense of awe and reverence in the
sanctuary. "Even when I dusted the Bible," she
explained, "I did it gently and with a feeling of
gratitude for what it was."

She was talking about holiness, the kind of
holiness that should be encountered and enhanced
with every service of worship. Webster reminds us
that *worship* means "to regard with great, even
extravagant respect."

Well, that holiness is hard to achieve when the
worship event is treated like a neighborhood soccer
game or a golden gloves boxing match. It's hard to
achieve when the prelude is punctuated with play-
by-play descriptions of the week's events. It's hard
to achieve when the pastoral prayer is a time to
search for mints to keep the kids happy. It's hard to
achieve when the morning anthem camouflages a
frantic scramble to locate the offering envelope.

And it's hard to achieve when the sermon constitutes a time to mutely arrange a mental calendar for the days ahead.

In chapter 1 we touched on the biblical concept of "knowing." We noted this is the highest level of communication that can exist between two people. Recently, evidence has come forth that there is no deeper level of vulnerability and understanding than that occurring immediately after a romantic interlude.

If you will pardon my boldness, I should like to compare that kind of open communication to an authentic worship experience.

In coming to God we drop all our pretenses, just like lovers. Barefoot before him, we are known and accepted just the way we are, just like lovers.

Thus freed from unwarranted expectations of worship (both on our part toward God and on what we imagine to be his part toward us), we shamelessly give and receive from one another, just like lovers.

It is a sacred experience, just like loving.

But how sacred would that loving be if we jabbered before it, involved ourselves in a rating process as it unfolded, and urgently fled as soon as it was concluded?

Worship, interwoven with reverence, enhances the holiness of God and heals the brokenness of persons.

THE MORE THE BETTER

Here is the icing on the cake. As our comprehension of holiness increases, those life-changing moments of katalysis multiply. That's right. The more we come to God, the more God comes to us! Or, at least, that is how we feel. God doesn't change his patterns at all. The more we draw near to him, the more capable we become of detecting his drawing near to us.

A distinguished British preacher often made this point by telling of a stroll through a London park. It was a breezy spring afternoon when he came upon a boy holding a string and staring off into an empty sky. Obviously he was flying a kite. But it had soared so high that it was now out of sight. In playful friendliness the preacher challenged the boy, "How do you know it's still up there?" Without hesitation the flyer replied, " 'Cause every once in a while I feel it tug."

Our contact with the holiness of God works the same way. We cannot see it. We cannot define it. But, with regular worship serving as the string, we find the more we hold on, the more we feel the tug.

It is the tug of a God who never stops caring.

LIKE A PARENT

They stole our hearts, that 1980 Olympic Hockey Team. With a combination of youthful daring and

bold exuberance they touched the button of
American pride in a manner not done for years.
When they tied Sweden they were a surprise. When
they beat Russia they were unbelievable. And when
they conquered Finland they were the toast of every
crossroad and hamlet in the land. The names of
Silk, Johnson, Eruzione, and Craig echoed over
coffee tables and punch clocks, check-out counters
and CB radios.

And oh that Craig, what a goalee he was! And
what a man. Two days before the showdown with
Russia, ABC told the story of the loss of his mother
to cancer two years before the games; how he had
gone on to school and become a star at Boston
University; how he had helped his dad hold the
home together. And when Jim McKay asked, "Who
is the greatest man you've ever known?" Craig
responded, "My dad!" So it should have been no
surprise when in the bedlam after the gold-clinching
victory, the camera focused on this handsome
young man, draped in an American flag, eyes
searching through the crowd. All about him people
were exploding with joy; the noise overwhelming.
But no one needed a microphone to feel the impact
of what he said as he stared imperviously through
the celebration into the stands. It had to be one of
the happiest moments of his life—one of those once-
in-a-lifetime suspensions between reality and a
dream. And Jim Craig said, "Where is my father?"

It was a tribute to the mutual respect and support of a healthy parent-child relationship.

May God bless each of our homes with a kindred condition.

So how does this kind of obvious understanding and affection compare to the relationship between every one of us and the God who fashioned our existence?

It is a great temptation to make comparisons. God helps every one of us conquer the tragedies of life, just like a parent. God hails our triumphs and grieves over our defeats, just like a parent. And when we lay hold of mountaintop experiences, those of us who believe make it a point to express our gratitude and thanks to the One who molded the moment.

The story could go on and on. God is friendly, like a parent. God is nice, like a parent. God is strong, like a parent. And God cares especially for me, like a parent.

And it all could be true. But it wouldn't be the complete truth. Furthermore, it could leave some of us terribly naive regarding the fullness of the parenthood of God.

As we withdraw from the siege of self-help hypnotics that has dominated the personal-religious scene over the last decade, we must avoid the pitfall of over-humanizing God. As noted earlier, God is still other, he is still sovereign, and he is still holy.

As such, his parenthood assumes dimensions foreign
to that of the natural parents with whom most of us
are acquainted.

UNFAIR BUT JUST

Certainly there is no area where this is more
obvious than in the impartiality of God's love. As
parent, God is just.

Now I want to be careful here that a line is drawn
between just and fair.

In their best-selling book *The Brethren*, Bob
Woodward and Scott Armstrong tell the story of
the highest court in our land. Closely perusing the
patterns of the supreme court they draw a
captivating picture of the enormous power resting in
just nine men. But what most fascinates me is the
way in which each of these judges carefully studies
the various cases brought before them. They know
the only way to do justice is with thorough
knowledge. Before they can determine what is right
they must know everything about the case.

Hypothetically, God as parent works the same
way with us. He knows us better than we know
ourselves. Possessing that all-inclusive knowledge, he
judges us.

This is where the difference between justness and
fairness comes into play. Life is not fair. We all
know joy and sorrow are not equally balanced over
the population of the world. They can't be when 10

percent of the people consume 90 percent of the
bounty. But God knows this, too, and ultimately
his justice will prevail. Life is not fair. God is not
fair. God is just.

I need only stand in the lobby of a children's
hospital and watch the progression of infants
besieged by pain and misery, and I quickly
determine that if this is all there is to life, God
stinks and I want nothing to do with him. But he
has promised through his word that this is not all
there is to it. "In my Father's house are many
rooms; if it were not so, would I have told you that
I go to prepare a place for you?" (John 14:2).

As parent, God knows everything there is to
know about every person who ever lived, and in the
end he shall use that knowledge to dispense his
justice unto eternity.

I think of the story Bill Russell, the former Boston
Celtic, tells about his grandfather and Kate, an old
mule. At that time, mules were the only means of
transportation available to the poor Louisiana
blacks.

> I could tell that Kate and the Old Man understood each
> other. One day I was walking along with them when
> Kate decided to go off and stand in a ditch. Being an
> honest mule, she had a stubborn, mulish personality, and
> she stood there with this determined look on her face. It
> was as if Kate were saying, "Okay, I got you now. We're
> going to do this my way." The Old Man did everything
> he could to get Kate back up on the road. I watched him

talk to her, and push, pull, shove and kick . . . a tough job, because there must have been nine hundred pounds of mule there. The Old Man would get Kate's front up on the road and be cooing in her ear, but when he walked around to pull up her tail end, the front would sidle back into the ditch again . . . so he'd take a deep breath and start over. I was taking all this in, and I couldn't believe that the Old Man didn't lose his temper.

After a long ordeal, Kate finally wound up back on the road. The Old Man looked exhausted and the mule must have taken some satisfaction from all the effort she'd cost him. She looked fresh and relaxed, standing there as warm and lazy as the country air. The Old Man leaned on Kate and rested there for a minute or two; then out of nowhere he hauled off and punched her with his bare fist. Whack, just once, right in the side of the neck. The thud was so loud I must have jumped a foot. The mule gently swayed back and forth groggily; then her front legs buckled and she collapsed to her knees. Then the hindquarters slowly buckled and settled down too. Kate looked all bent and contorted, like a squatting camel, as she sat there with that vacant stare in her eyes. I was dumbstruck. Right in front of my eyes the Old Man had knocked out a mule with one punch.

The Old Man knew he'd have been in big trouble if he'd knocked out that mule down in the ditch, so he waited until it didn't cost him anything. Then he relieved his frustration and gave Kate something to think about.[1]

The just parent works in a similar manner. We may think, like Kate, that we've got things going our way, that we've taken control, that we hold the power to determine our destiny. Don't believe it for

a minute. God, the just parent, knows everything
we've ever done and shall one day exact
accountability from us.

Recall the words from Genesis regarding the cities
of Sodom and Gomorrah:

> Because the outcry against Sodom and Gomorrah is great
> and their sin is very grave, I will go down to see whether
> they have done altogether according to the
> outcry which has come to me; and if not, I will know.
>
> Genesis 18:20-21

We may fool our natural parents, and certainly all
of us did at one time or another, but we never fool
our heavenly parent. He knows each of us
inclusively and shall exercise judgment anchored in
that knowledge.

FORGIVENESS AS A CONDITION OF EXISTENCE

If God the parent were solely interested in justice,
we would all have cause for alarm. But a second
characteristic of God as parent exists in which we
find the secret to our sanity. God the parent is just.
He is also forgiving.

Undoubtedly P. T. Forsyth perceived this thesis
when he sought to strike a balance between the
faith and work of the Son.

> We cannot put too much into that word Father. It is the
> sum and marrow of all Christian divinity. But we may
> easily put in too little. That is what we all do in some

way. Only once has enough been put into it. And that
was in the faith and work of Christ. "Father, forgive
them." "Father" . . . that was His faith. "Forgive them"
. . . that was His work.[2]

This is the great paradox of the Christian faith.
We are a *known* people, naked before God; we are,
at the same time, a *forgiven* people, forever wrapped
in his love. This forgiveness is an existent condition
constantly flowing from God the parent. He loves
us more than we can mess up.

Unfortunately, that is a tough lesson for many
Christians to learn. Confused by the multiple
influences of a works-righteousness society and an
overemphasis on the final judgment of God, we
spend a lot of time doing one of two things: (1)
separating ourselves from the world, trying to avoid
all possible contact with sin, or (2) totally denying a
relationship with God because we feel too guilty to
deserve his love.

What we must understand is that we never
deserve his love. It is given freely. And it is greater
than all our sin.

DROPPING THE LOAD

There are few experiences in our society more
guilt-laden and failure-convincing than the process
of divorce. It often leaves scars that never heal.

It was after his first divorce that Bill Coffin, now
the Senior Minister at Riverside Church in New

York, had an encounter with an old friend that
isolates our tendency to cling to guilt loads even in
the face of forgiveness. Coffin had endured the
divorce by himself. Like many people, he didn't feel
like sharing his pain with his friends. Thus, while
walking with Abraham Heschel, the noted New
York rabbi, Coffin was stunned when his wise old
friend brought it up.

Slipping his hand under my arm he began, "I
understand, my friend, that you have been through much
suffering."

"That's right, Father Abraham, it's been hell. It still is."

"You should have called me," he said.

"You were in Los Angeles all summer."

"You still could have called me."

"Well, I didn't want to bother you. Besides, I had other
friends I could talk to and I don't like talking about such
things over the phone."

"That was a mistake, I could have helped you."

Irked by his self assurance I stopped and faced him.
"All right, how could you have helped me?"

As I had seen him do so often he raised his shoulders
and his hands, palms up. "I would have told you about
my father, the great Hasidic rabbi, blessed be his
memory, who too was divorced. You see, you Christians
are so vexed by your perfectionism. It is always your
undoing."

He continued to talk in this vein, and I felt the tears
starting down my cheeks. He was so right. And it was
nice that a Jew was reminding a Christian that his
salvation lay not in being sinless, but in accepting his
forgiveness."[3]

Yes, God is just. And, even more important, God
is forgiving.

WE NOW HAVE ALL WE NEED TO COPE

It was 1969 and I was sitting in the front pew of a
tiny country church in Chadwick, Illinois. I was
there as the guest preacher for the week and at the
moment we were concluding the traditional rousing
round of singing before the message for the evening.
The host minister stood up and proceeded to
introduce the soloist for the night. He told how
hard she had worked in the church; grieved over
the loss of one of her children in World War II, and
recalled the recent passing of her faithful spouse of
over seventy years. Then she sang. She was nearly
ninety years old and her singing voice was long
since gone. Her song, a hymn by Charles H.
Gabriel, was beautiful.

> Why should I feel discouraged,
> Why should the shadows come,
> Why should my heart be lonely,
> And long for heav'n and home,
>
> When Jesus is my portion?
> My constant friend is He:
> His eye is on the sparrow,
> And I know He watches me.

Like the best of our natural parents, God is not
only just and forgiving, he is also our provider. He

meets us at the point of our need and gives us everything we need to cope with this life. As the author of those fantastic "moments of katalysis," he supplies shelter, power, and purpose for every circumstance we might engage.

This is the power of the words of Matthew. They are words that reveal the intimacy of the parent-child relationship between all who would call upon his name and the God who thoroughly knows his people, shields their nakedness with his forgiveness, and celebrates their *joy* while providing their sustenance.

> Ask, and it will be given you; seek and you will find; knock, and it will be opened to you. For every one who asks receives, and he who seeks finds, and to him who knocks it will be opened. Or what man of you, if his son asks him for a loaf, will give him a stone? Or if he asks for a fish, will give him a serpent? If you then, who are evil, know how to give good gifts to your children, how much more will your Father who is in heaven give good things to those who ask Him!
>
> Matthew 7:7—11

THE ABUSE OF PRIVILEGE

But look at what we have done with the gifts. We have filled the rivers with industrial waste and fogged the air with putrid chemicals. We have massacred the animals and decimated the foliage. We have constructed massive, unmanageable cities, only to abandon them to rats and ruin. And we

have separated God's children into haves and have-
nots, destroying their dignity and perpetuating their
indifference.

All things considered, God, the parent, has cause
to be upset.

I think of the lad who received a sparkling new
bicycle for his birthday. The first night he parked it
by his bed and his father felt a surge of warmth
when he witnessed his son's contented sleep. Two
weeks later the bike was relegated to the garage.
Three months later dad nearly ran over it because it
was left in the driveway. And six months later the
father was flabbergasted to see the boy stretched out
in the middle of the family room enviously gazing at
the bicycle section of the Sears catalog.

God, the parent, has provided. But we, the
children, have neglected. Thus now, more than ever
before, we need a consultant who can guide our
steps. We need a helpmate who can evoke the best
from deep within us. We need that special someone
who can cause us to change while catering to our
calamity. We need God who will help us modify the
present as we magnify the future.

In section three we will meet him.

III.
Now and Then:
A Look at Our
Friend and Future

In John Cheever's short story, "Goodbye, My Brother," he paints the picture of a perfectionist destined to live in obscurity. So high are the expectations of this man that he finds it impossible to maintain a relationship with any person, place, or thing. Nothing is good enough. Late in the story, Lawrence, the brother, is walking with his sister on the beach.

"I don't like it here," he said blandly, without raising his eyes. "I'm going to sell my equity in the house to Chaddy. I didn't expect to have a good time. The only reason I came back was to say goodbye."

I let him get ahead again and I walked behind him, looking at his shoulders and thinking of all the goodbyes he had made. When Father drowned, he went to church and said goodbye to Father. It was only three years later that he concluded that Mother was frivolous and said goodbye to her. In his freshman year at college, he had been very good friends with his roommate, but the man drank too much, and at the beginning of the spring term

Lawrence changed roommates and said goodbye to his friend. When he had been in college for two years, he concluded that the atmosphere was too sequestered and he said goodbye to Yale. He enrolled at Columbia and got his law degree there, but he found his employer dishonest, and at the end of six months he said goodbye to a good job. He married Ruth in City Hall and said goodbye to the Protestant Episcopal Church; they went to live on a back street in Tuckahoe and said goodbye to the middle class. In 1938, he went to Washington to work as a government lawyer, saying goodbye to private enterprise, but after eight months in Washington he concluded that the Roosevelt administration was sentimental and he said goodbye to it. They left Washington for a suburb of Chicago, where he said goodbye to his neighbors, one by one, on counts of drunkenness, boorishness, and stupidity. He said goodbye to Chicago and went to Kansas; he said goodbye to Kansas and went to Cleveland. Now he had said goodbye to Cleveland and come East again, stopping at Laud's Head long enough to say goodbye to the sea.[1]

God, the present friend, never says goodbye.

If a single characteristic dominates our culture, it is mobility. Largely influenced by corporate manipulation, the average American family makes a move once every three years. Just a few days ago I received a letter from a woman who was making her fourth move within eighteen months. Needless to say, she was frazzled.

The end effect of all this bouncing about is an increasingly defensive, well-insulated individual who is careful to establish only first-layer friendships and is determined to remain invulnerable to the pain of what I choose to call "phileo-interruptus," the collapse of friendship. It's just not worth the effort to get close to anybody because the odds on external circumstance destroying the situation are just too high. Why go through the pain? Why risk the hours of emptiness? Why love and lose? Why fear goodbye?

The world of faith has not avoided this challenge. Like any other in-depth relationship, our homogeneity with God suffers from a fear of termination. The possibility of playing the fool by investing one's self in a connection with an undefinable being renders most of us cautious and some of us downright hostile.

But a friendship with God is a friendship like no other.

Unlike those moored in the harbors of humanity, a friendship with God is never threatened by geographic relocation. No matter where we are, God is always accessible.

ALWAYS WITHIN REACH

I consider it one of the telltale marks of the uneasiness of our time that we are currently swamped with "convenience stores." Banking on the insatiable American penchant for comfort and speed, the very existence of these "pay a little more

. . . get it a little easier" outlets reveals a need for instant gratification. It's another mark of the "children of the moment" mentioned in chapter 1. We want what we want when we want it, and if we have to pay more for the pleasure, so be it. Just make sure we are never forced to do without.

We worship accessibility. Yet many of us fail to note the only constantly accessible resource we have, the friendship of God.

Blitzed by the loss of a loved one, when it seems no one can care enough or do enough, God, the present friend, is there.

Confused by the amoral indifference of the world of business, certain no one remembers how hard you have worked and how much you have sacrificed, God, the present friend, is there.

Baffled by a siege of illness the cause and justice of which is totally incomprehensible, God, the present friend, is there.

Promises James, "Draw near to God and he will draw near to you" (James 4:8).

UNBELIEVABLE ACCESS

On April 27, 1978, I was awakened at 3:00 A.M. with the news that Shiloh Church was on fire. An arsonist had set four fires in the building, and when I arrived the flames had totally consumed the lower level interior. The firemen contained the fire itself, but smoke damage destroyed everything in the building. It was a mess and an overwhelming challenge.

The congregation met that challenge. On June 10, 1979, we dedicated the completely renewed edifice with former President Gerald R. Ford as our keynote speaker and guest of honor.

I won't soon forget our negotiations with the thirty-eighth President to get him to come to Shiloh Church. To begin with, it was a pipe dream, one of those crazy things where you figure you can't lose by trying. We didn't even have an address, so we sent the letter general delivery to Gerald Ford, Palm Springs. Five weeks passed and there was no answer so we sent a second, identical letter, registered. Three weeks passed and there was still no response, so we began to consider our second choice.

Then came the letter. No stamp. Just his signature in the upper right hand corner and a beautiful gold seal on the back.

The office went bananas.

Still, I remember thinking, "Here's the rejection, but at least we got a fancy piece of stationery." I was wrong. Inside was a note from the President's secretary explaining our stationery did not contain a telephone number and giving us theirs so we might discuss the matter further.

We cheered with delight. The key was that telephone number. I understand it is very hard to get. But there it was. And it was saying, "I'm

available, call me!" It was making the former
President of the United States available to me. It
was a heady moment indeed.

It was unbelievable access.

But in comparison to the act of God in Christ
two thousand years ago, that Presidential letter is a
pittance. When God became man in Jesus of
Nazareth, it was the supreme act of friendship for
all persons. It was the release of a telephone
number, an agreement to accessibility, an unceasing
proclamation, *"I am available . . . call me!"*

But like all friendships, ours with God is a two-
way street. To restate an earlier position, the more
we come to God, the more he comes to us. It makes
me think of the two men who passed in a
restaurant. Obviously friends, one said to the other,
"Why haven't you called me?" The retort makes the
point: "Your phone has a dial on it."

> Seek the Lord while he may be found,
>   call upon him while he is near;
> let the wicked forsake his way,
>   and the unrighteous man his thoughts;
> let him return to the Lord, that he may have
>   mercy on him,
> and to our God, for he will
>   abundantly pardon.
>
> Isaiah 55:6–7

IT ALL ADDS UP

God, the present friend, is readily available. He is
also deliberate. This is one of those areas that needs

special understanding. In the face of disaster and
trauma, most of us ask, "How can God let this
happen?" Yet, when we examine God's role as
present friend, we develop a new perspective on
catastrophe.

In his book *The Problem of Pain*, C. S. Lewis
describes the need for natural order in the life
process. Certain laws (such as that of gravity and
our dependence on oxygen) are unavoidable. They
establish order and some degree of predictability in
what otherwise would be chaos. Unfortunately,
under certain circumstances these same laws can be
as destructive as they are creative. If you doubt
that, consider jumping off a ten-story building.
Thus, our challenge is to accept the pain with the
pleasure. Lewis puts it this way:

> So it is with the life of souls in a world: fixed laws,
> consequences unfolding by causal necessity, the whole
> natural order, are at once the limits within which their
> common life is confined and also the sole condition
> under which any such life is possible. Try to exclude the
> possibility of suffering which the order of nature and the
> existence of free-wills involve, and you find that you have
> excluded life itself.[2]

So we come to understand that the gift of life
brings with it the possibility for disaster. You can't
have one without the other.

When that giant DC-10 lifted off the runway at
O'Hare airport not so long ago everybody on board
was fortunate to be en route to sunny California.

But when it dropped an engine and began a plunge to destruction, those same people were rendered unfortunate victims, with no regard for personalities.

When the honeymoon couple played on the Jamaican beach in the glittering rays of the Carribean sun, they were considered privileged. But when that same climate generated 150-mile-per-hour winds that picked up the azure surf and slammed it into the honeymoon cottage burying both of them under a pile of rubble, they were considered hapless prey to an indifferent destroyer.

When a four-year-old boy cut his fingers on a piece of glass only to watch his blood coagulate and seal the wound, he was considered the recipient of God's wisdom through the miracle of the human body. But two years later when that same blood developed an imbalance between the white corpuscles and the red, he was considered the cursed carrier of leukemia.

The laws of nature call for a delicate balance. When it is broken, it is not a matter of reward and punishment. It is a matter of cause and effect.

HE HAS A PIECE OF THE ACTION

The importance of God, the present friend, is found in the fact that we never have to face disaster alone. Here Emil Brunner brings us light.

> The living God does not, like the divinity of Plato, stand
> above the changing temporal process, but He enters into
> it, indeed He even steps into History. As the Holy and
> Loving one He takes part in the historical process, with
> an infinite interest in what men do and leave undone.[3]

Hence, our deliberate God, who structured this life within the bounds of fixed laws, leaps into the midst of the event—first, in the form of a living and dying Christ; second, as a resurrected Lord and an ever-present Spirit.

In this capacity God feels what we feel, knows what we know, dreams what we dream, and experiences all that we experience. He practices compassion in its fullest sense. Not only to the point where he feels sorry for his children, but to the point where he virtually shares our frustration, endures our pain, and undergoes our emptiness.

THE HIGH COST OF FRIENDSHIP

There are two kinds of people who dominate the life of the average minister. The first are those who can neither be satisfied nor silenced. Always complaining, they are the folk to whom one would like to remark, just once, "Don't talk to me again until you think of something positive." The second are those who leave a wide margin for error and never stop working. Any time the door is open they are there, ready, willing, able.

Sue Loomis and Carol Taylor are type two. I

share this story with their consent.

Not only are these two superworkers, they are also superfriends. During the reconstruction of the church, people would frequently snap pictures after worship just to record progress. In many of those pictures one can see Sue and Carol standing in the sanctuary chatting with each other.

Just a few months ago, Carol, who is a nurse, was attending a training meeting when she happened to put her hand under her chin. It was a move destined to bring shock and fear. She felt a lump. Not a big lump, but a lump.

A trip to the doctor led her to outpatient surgery at a local hospital. I arrived in the waiting room just moments after the doctor had shared his diagnosis with Carol's husband Jim and (who else?) Sue.

The diagnosis? Hodgkin's disease.

I remember a sudden vacuum in my stomach. Had we not been in a waiting room I probably would have cried. Jim got up to go in and see Carol, and it was then that I saw the look on Sue's face. Pain, shock, disappointment, and incredulity all combined in a timid tilt of the head and eyes at once moist and warm. She didn't say anything. She didn't have to. She was not feeling sorry for Carol, she was virtually sharing the dilemma.

This is the high cost of real friendship. It could be said that every friend multiplies the possibilities of disaster. But it could also be said those same friendships bring a good deal more joy than pain.

Carol has learned she was fortunate to catch the disease in its earliest stage and is now undergoing regular treatment. The whole church rejoices at her progress, but I seriously question whether any of us feel it quite the same as Sue. Now the disease is in remission and Sue and Carol are again active in all phases of church life.

Like the true friend who meets our dumb struck awe in the face of disaster with a speechless tear of her own, so God literally participates in the life events of his children. Having deliberately established a relationship of love with all who communicate with him, God does not bail out when the going gets tough any more than our natural friends would abandon us in the time of need. To the contrary, at those times, he draws nearer and, in the midst of our despair, the present friend gives us hope.

RAINBOWS IN THE RAIN

Few people would have recognized these truths any faster than Leslie Weatherhead. As the pastor of the London City Temple during World War II, he developed the capacity to recognize God's continuing victories in the midst of costly and devastating circumstances.

> Gash the earth with your railway cutting and Nature at once gets busy on the scar, and covers it with not only

the kind of green grass which grew on the surrounding fields, but with tender violets and primroses which would not grow until a cleft in the earth provided shelter from the north wind. With evil intent men crucified the Son of God, and within six weeks other men were preaching about the Cross as the instrument of salvation. They hardly once referred to it as the crime of man.
They—with a daring almost alarming—spoke of it as a redemptive act of God.[4]

And then again,

There is a will of God within evil circumstances, and let every sufferer who may happen to read these lines realize that if he makes the right reaction to these circumstances, the ultimate will of God will be reached *as effectively as if he had not been ill.* God would not allow cancer if *of itself* it had the power to defeat him.[5]

Without the rain . . . there could be no rainbow. And so this deliberate, present friend has a way of planting violets and primroses in the scars of nature. If the balance of nature is to continue, he will not prevent cause and effect dilemmas. But, as the most faithful and present friend we can ever know, he can come to us in our times of trial and give us the strength not only to cope with the moment but to find joy in its midst.

Alan Walker conveys this idea with a story about the author Charles Lamb in *God, the Disturber.*

Charles Lamb, a famous figure in English literature, came home one day from his accountant position to find that his sister Mary, while mentally unbalanced, had murdered their parents. Friends urged Charles to put her in an institution. He refused, giving up his position to care for her, depending entirely upon his writing. For twenty-seven years he looked after her. He would not leave her alone. Asked after her death how he carried the continual strain, he said, "I could not have kept it on for a year, or even a month, if I had thought of it as a year or a month. I was able to endure it because I took the days one at a time, happy when Mary was happy, and seeking God's help when she was disturbed.[6]

I see that as a perfect illustration of the faithful friend, not only on the part of Mr. Lamb (who was also a brother), but on behalf of God (who is concurrently parent and friend). Lamb made it a point to *be there* for his beleaguered sister. God made it a point to *be there* for both of them.

God, the present friend, makes himself readily available to his people, then deliberately involves himself in their living.

POSSIBILITY IN THE PALM OF PAIN

In the summer immediately after the fire at Shiloh Church, I often found myself torn between a need to feel the support of others and the need to be completely alone. I suppose it was an effect of the pressure. I needed people, but I was sick of them. One afternoon I had a late appointment in Cincinnati and as it was concluded early, I decided to go to a Reds game by myself. That may sound

like a weird way to get away from folks, planting
yourself in the middle of 30,000 of them, but it
worked. I managed a seat in the green section of the
left field stands, and though I was surrounded with
partisans, I was alone. The phone couldn't ring. No
one could ask me about the building. And I felt
reasonably secure from those *quid pro quo*
conversationalists who seem to abound when
pressure is at its peak.

I remember sitting there wondering, "Why me?
Why did I get this horrendous task? Why did some
clown set Shiloh Church on fire?" And even as I
was musing about my misfortune I heard the guy in
front of me telling a friend about his son and
birthdays. Only a parent could feel the punch of
what he said.

Apparently he had a six-year-old who was really
into birthdays—not just his own but that of
everybody in the house. When his mother had a
birthday, she was awakened to the little guy
standing by the bed, with a box of detergent
wrapped in toilet paper, singing, "Happy birthday to
you." When it was dad's turn, he told of the child
bringing him a nail—a single old nail—and singing
again. And when the cat's number came up, he got
a little paper bag full of kitty litter. At every turn,
the boy produced some gift that revealed his
knowledge of the receiver. "Ain't that something?"
he said to his buddy, and they went back to
watching the game.

It was more something than he knew. I sat there and reasoned: if a little boy can be so deliberate about what he gives to those he loves, how much more deliberate is God about the things he allows in the lives of those he loves? He never gives us a challenge we can't handle. And he never misses a day in which he doesn't give us yet again the tools we need to encounter his will.

Sure, we had a fire. But we also had an architect as the president of council, a real estate developer as the chairman of renewal, a vice-president of the bank to handle the insurance claim, several students of interior design on the planning committee, and a committed congregation and staff more than capable of meeting the crisis.

I can't remember who won the Reds game. I guess I did, because I walked out of that stadium convinced yet again that God was—and is—and always will be my friend.

So informed, I welcomed the future.

PAVILIONED IN SPLENDOR

Twenty-five centuries have passed since David sat on a hill overlooking Jerusalem and wrote these words, but he could have written them last week from the observation deck of the Empire State Building in New York or the Sears Tower in Chicago or the Transamerica Building in San Francisco, or Winter's Bank in Dayton.

I think of God, and I moan;
    I meditate, and my spirit faints.
Thou dost hold my eyelids from closing;
    I am so troubled that I cannot speak.
I consider the days of old,
    I remember the years long ago.
I commune with my heart in the night;
    I meditate and search my spirit:
"Will the Lord spurn for ever,
    and never again be favorable?
Has his steadfast love for ever ceased?
    Are his promises at an end for all time?
Has God forgotten to be gracious?
    Has he in anger shut up his compassion?"
                                    Psalm 77:3–9

Obviously David was uptight. But he couldn't
have been any more uptight than most Americans
are today. Staring at runaway inflation, humiliated
by a bearded guru and a handful of fanatic
students, taunted by Soviet expansionism, and
discouraged by the lack of clear political choices,
we, too, could cry out, "Will the Lord spurn for
ever, and never again be favorable?"

But to do so would be to confess our
nearsightedness and uncover a shallow faith. It
would be to admit our lack of confidence in both
the word of God and his continuing love. It would
be to deny God as our future.

David figured it out. Just a few chapters after his
defeatist's lament he comes back with these words:

Before the mountains were brought forth,
　or ever thou hadst formed the earth and the world,
from everlasting to everlasting thou art God.
Psalm 90:2

It was his way of handing himself over to the will of
God, the continuing handiwork of the Creator, the
justice of the parent, and the compassion of the
present friend. It was the repentant king's method
of announcing, "God is in charge here and I trust
his providence."

As I survey the current mind-set of the Christian
world it comes to me that it is time to repeat that
proclamation. It is time to consider the faithfulness
of our Maker, to recall the rainbow covenant
between God and Noah, and to sense again the
fabulous promise of the borrowed but vacated tomb.

—Our God lives.

—Our God loves.

—Our God looks after his own.

The future belongs to him.

In light of that liberating truth some basic
attitudinal changes are in order for those of us who
have made a life-style of "getting to know who?"

WHAT WE ARE FOR RATHER THAN WHAT WE ARE AGAINST

God as future calls us to live creatively rather
than defensively.

More than thirty years ago *Atlantic* magazine
published an article by Archibald MacLeish entitled
"The Conquest of America" in which he put forth
a prophecy we have lived to realize. MacLeish
maintained that our overwhelming fixation on the
actions of Russia would benumb our greatest
national asset, our belief in the dignity and worth of
the individual. As he explained, the problem is a
matter of posture.

> A people who have been real to themselves because they
> were *for* something cannot continue to be real to
> themselves when they find they are merely *against*
> something.[7]

In other words, if our lives are controlled by what
others do, we can never pioneer in what we do.
Defensive counter-development saps the energy
needed for creative extension.

Since 7:08 A.M., December 7, 1941, our country
has been consumed by what it is against at the
expense of its creative edge. To be sure, there have
been moments of brilliance, but they, too, were
generated more by what we didn't want than by
what we did.

Consider the development of nuclear power. Now
it is held up as an agent of hope in the ballooning
battle with energy. Please remember its origin was in
response to foreign aggression.

Or what of the venerated conquest of space? We

hail it as our greatest achievement, a classic example of American technology and courage. We forget it was begun by a predecessor called Sputnik.

And today, we wrestle with inflation, once again dominated by what we fear more than what we treasure. The challenge is to see beyond what we might lose to that which we might gain.

A life-style structured on defense is a life-style in conflict with the call of God as future.

THE PROMISED PRESENCE

It couldn't be made more clear than in chapter 6 of the Book of Exodus. The Israelites are in bondage in Egypt. Their dignity is demolished, their pride crushed, and their confidence in themselves as a people is so weak that when God calls them to shake their bonds and return to the promised land, they don't have the guts to do it. They are a broken people. Gone is their fierce independence. Gone is their trust in their leaders. Gone is their tenacity in the face of oppression. They are willing to remain slaves to current condition. Sound familiar?

But the word of the Lord comes to Moses, and it is a word that always comes to those who deposit the future with God.

I have heard the groaning of the people of Israel . . . and
I have remembered my covenant. . . . "I am the Lord,

and I will bring you out from under the burdens of the
Egyptians, and I will deliver you from their bondage . . . ,
and I will take you for my people, and I will be your
God."

Exodus 6:5-7a

Now those people were not unlike most of us.
They had adjusted to their way of life and learned
how to handle their oppressors. They really didn't
want to change. Furthermore, in order to escape the
Egyptians they had to flee into the desert. That was
ridiculous.

But God, as future, often calls us to what appears
to be ridiculous. Need I remind you that same
desert is now the key to the Suez Canal and the
heartland of the world's oil supply?

The question is this: Do we trust God's
providence enough to engage the future creatively
or are we consumed with returning to the good old
days and charting our course by the moves of our
adversary?

Carl Braaten dwells on the same theme.

The God whom Jesus proclaimed is not the guarantor of
the status quo. He is the power of the future pressing for
radical conversion of the present.[8]

In this light, God as future has no use for those
who would rally the wagons in a circle and defend
our present style of life. He does have a dramatic

use for those who hail his guidance and creatively engage tomorrow. He does have a use for those who recognize the value of the individual as a unique and unrepeatable miracle of God. He does have a use for those who freely receive their moments of katalysis and for those who comprehend that any form of authoritarianism jams the lines of communication between God and his people. MacLeish wisely declares:

> The one force which can claim the revolutionary title in the world we live in, the one force which can claim to move in the direction of life, is the force that Jefferson put into words. Later Americans have, it is true, betrayed that force, both in terms and actions. Its vocabulary has been appropriated again and again for private advantage. Its victories have been corrupted by hypocrisy and cynicism and selfishness. Its articles of faith have been made the catechism of a faithless materialism. Its central concept of the dignity of the individual, grown cancerous on occasion, has swollen to the morbid and malignant figure of irresponsible and grasping power—the "rugged individual" whom some still think of as American. But though the hope has been betrayed and forgotten in one generation and another, the living seed remains: the seed remains and grows. It is this seed, this influence, this force, this force of revolution, which is the living thing in the Republic. Without it, the United States is so much land, so many people, such an accumulation of wealth. With it the United States is a stage upon the journey of mankind.[9]

Today, as the free world teeters on the brink of economic suicide, God calls Christians to the center of that stage, not to rail against the purge of Afghanistan or the confusion of Iran or even the malnutrition visited upon our economy by cheap dollars and exorbitant prices. No, God calls us to center stage to establish yet again

—Our commitment to individual dignity,
—Our willingness to sacrifice pleasure in pursuit of promise,
—Our ability to accept risk as a precedent to growth,
—Our trust in God that frees us from postures of defense and hate to those of creativity and love.

Like the huddled orphans of Israel chaffing beneath the chains of the Egyptians, we must stop licking our wounds, turn to the guidance of God, and willingly invade the desert.

If that means reduced credit and higher interest, so be it.

If that means cutback in conveniences and greater dependency on one another, so be it.

And if it means the power of the populace brought to focus upon the indifferences of corporate profit and the blindness of unionism, so be it.

God as future forever challenges his people to center their lives on the hope of what could be, and not on the despair of what actually exists.

WHO'S ON FIRST?

He also calls us to put truth in first place rather than second.

This is a matter of allegiances and, unfortunately, for many of us our first allegiance is to comfort and security. Only when these are guaranteed do we direct our attention to the injustice of hopelessness of others.

I am reminded of that feeling one experiences when, seated at a dining table, he asks that the condiments be passed only to observe the person beside him freely salting his potatoes and peppering his beef before honoring the initial request.

I think of God. For more than two thousand years we have held his requests.

—Thou shalt have no other gods before me.

—Remember the sabbath, keep it holy.

—Thou shalt not kill.

You know the list. But somehow we have managed to indulge ourselves on virtually every count. It is as if we have explained: "As soon as I get my fortune, then I will stop worshiping bounty and truly worship you." "As soon as I get relaxed and enjoy some recreation, then I will worry about the sabbath." "As soon as I establish my political system and gain geographic control, then I shall stop killing."

Who are we kidding? If the truth of God is valid,

it must come first, not second. If we accept the
dignity of every individual as proof of our creation
in the image of God, we cannot look the other way
when millions starve or friendly dictators use torture
to reinforce their regimes.

If we believe inflation is perpetuated by increased
spending, we cannot be satisfied to blame the
government yet, for example, buy a boat.

And if we believe God is sovereign, holy, creator,
parent, friend, and future, we cannot go on
structuring our lives on the defense of our excesses
at the expense of our possibilities.

> If my people who are called by my name humble
> themselves, and pray and seek my face, and turn from
> their wicked ways, then I will hear from heaven, and
> will forgive their sin and heal their land.
>
> 2 Chronicles 7:14

The point of convergence remains the individual.
We might generally observe that the way of God is
not synonymous with the way of the United States;
in this instance, though, they are perfectly matched.
The backbone of this country is the dignity and
worth of individuals; so also the nerve center of
God as future is his commitment to interact with
every living soul on a one-to-one basis. Without
God's help we created the mess now bewildering us.
With his help we can renew our hope and conquer
the quandary.

Echoing Isaiah's observation, "I am the first and I am the last: besides me there is no God" (44:6*b*), Carl Braaten again clarifies the challenge.

> Christians remember the past hopefully as that which is reconciled to the present from the power of their common future. The power of God to raise the dead includes the power to gather up the broken, unfulfilled past into a new creation, so that at the end "God may be everyone to everyone."[10]

Paul says the same thing, only his problem is a lot easier for most of us to feel. Trapped in a Roman jail, haunted by the certainty of his fast-approaching death, and surrounded by fellow prisoners who had long surrendered hope, the apostle gave us some of the most stirring words in the Bible. I think of them often when I note despair in the life of a fellow believer.

I think of them in my office when a couple stares vacantly each at the other and asks, "What's left?"

I think of them at bedside when a patient under siege whispers, "I can't take it anymore. I'm going to quit."

And I think of them as I look into the eighties and sense the dramatic changes we must all be willing to make.

> I have learned, in whatever state I am, to be content. I know how to be abased, and I know how to abound; in any and all circumstances I have learned the secret of

facing plenty and hunger, abundance and want. I can do
all things in him who strengthens me.

Philippians 4:11*b*-13

That is the power of the One who is our friend
and future.

NOTES

Chapter I

1. Emil Brunner, *Our Faith* (New York: Charles Scribner's Sons, 1936), p. 21.

2. Mark Link, S. J., *He Is the Still Point of the Turning World* (Niles, Illinois: Argus Communications, 1971), p. 76.

3. Marilee Zdenek and Marge Champion, *God Is a Verb!* (Waco, Texas: Word Books, 1974), p. 18.

4. Paul Tillich, *Systematic Theology,* 3 vols. (Chicago: University of Chicago Press, 1951), 1:252-3.

5. Aaron Stern, M. D., *Me: The Narcissistic American* (New York: Ballantine Books, 1979), p. 7.

6. Leslie D. Weatherhead, *The Christian Agnostic* (Nashville: Abingdon, 1965), p. 72.

Chapter II

1. William Russell, *Second Wind* (New York: Random House, 1979), p. 7.

2. Peter Taylor Forsyth, *God the Holy Father* (London: Independent Press Ltd., 1897), p. 5.

3. William Sloane Coffin, *Once to Every Man* (New York: Atheneum, 1977), p. 289.

Chapter III

1. John Cheever, *The Stories of John Cheever* (New York: Alfred Knopf, 1978), p. 18.

2. C. S. Lewis, *The Problem of Pain* (London: Fontana Books, 1957), p. 22.

3. Emil Brunner, *The Christian Doctrine of God* (New York: Charles Scribner's Sons, 1936), p. 271.

4. Leslie D. Weatherhead, *The Will of God* (Nashville: Abingdon, 1944), p. 31.

5. Ibid., p. 22.

6. Alan Walker, *God, the Disturber* (Waco, Texas: Word Books, 1973), p. 47.

7. Archibald MacLeish, "The Conquest of America," *The Atlantic,* March 1980, p. 35.

8. Carl Braaten, *The Future of God* (New York: Harper & Row, 1969), p. 69.

9. MacLeish, "The Conquest of America," p. 39.

10. Braaten, *The Future of God*, p. 81.